WELCOMF

MW00456970

TRAVEL

by **VAN**

PLANNER & DIARY

THIS JOURNAL BELONGS TO:

INSIDE...
- Map and Visual Planner
- Trip-at-a-glance Planner
- Bucket List
- Trip Budget Planner
- Itinerary Details - Flights, Accommodation and Transfers
- 5-week day planner
- Packing List Generator
- Common Conversions
- Winter and Summer Time Zones
- Fuel and Expense Logs
- Reversible 32-day Journal

If found, please return to:

_____

_____

_____

TRAVEL
New Zealand
VISUAL PLANNER by VAN
North Island

How to use...
List your personal places of interest
in the box, then draw a line to the area
...like this!   *Auckland Sailing*

Kaitaia

Paihia

Whangarei

Auckland

Hamilton

Tauranga

Rotorua

Gisborne

New Plymouth

Napier

Palmerston
North

Wellington

TRAVEL
New Zealand by VAN
VISUAL PLANNER
South Island

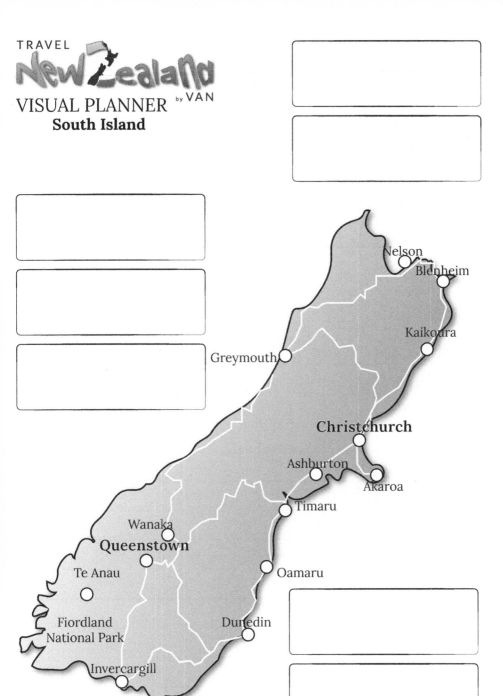

Nelson

Blenheim

Kaikoura

Greymouth

Christchurch

Ashburton

Akaroa

Timaru

Wanaka

Queenstown

Te Anau

Oamaru

Fiordland
National Park

Dunedin

Invercargill

TRIP AT A GLANCE by VAN

WHERE:

WHEN:

WHO:

WHAT:

WHY:

HOW:

TRAVEL
New Zealand
BUCKET LIST by VAN

Area: _____

ESSENTIAL: _____

_____

_____

_____

_____

_____

_____

_____

_____

_____

_____

_____

_____

NICE TO DO: _____

_____

_____

_____

_____

_____

_____

...IF WE HAVE TIME: _____

_____

_____

TRAVEL
New Zealand
BUCKET LIST *by* VAN

Area:

ESSENTIAL:

NICE TO DO:

...IF WE HAVE TIME:

TRAVEL

BUCKET LIST by VAN

Area:

ESSENTIAL:

NICE TO DO:

...IF WE HAVE TIME:

TRAVEL
New Zealand
BUCKET LIST by VAN

Area:

ESSENTIAL:

NICE TO DO:

...IF WE HAVE TIME:

TRAVEL

NeW Zealand
BUCKET LIST by VAN

Area: _____

ESSENTIAL: _____

_____

_____

_____

_____

_____

_____

_____

_____

_____

_____

_____

_____

NICE TO DO: _____

_____

_____

_____

_____

_____

_____

_____

_____

...IF WE HAVE TIME: _____

_____

_____

TRAVEL
New Zealand
BUCKET LIST by VAN

Area: _____

ESSENTIAL: _____

_____

_____

_____

_____

_____

_____

_____

_____

_____

_____

_____

_____

NICE TO DO: _____

_____

_____

_____

_____

_____

_____

...IF WE HAVE TIME: _____

_____

_____

TRIP BUDGET by VAN

Currency:

Expense	Budget	Actual	Notes
TRANSPORT			
Airfares			
Car Hire			
Gas/Fuel			
Fares			
Misc			
OTHER			
Visas			
Insurance			
Phone/Sim Card			
ACCOMMODATION			
Hotels/Hostels			
BnB's			
Campsites			
Misc			
SIGHTS & ACTIVITIES			
Tickets			
Total page 1			

Currency:

Expense	Budget	Actual	Notes
SHOPPING *buy here*			
Luggage			
Apps			
Maps/Guides			
SHOPPING *buy there*			
Souvenirs			
Clothes			
Tax-Free			
Misc			
FOOD & DRINK			
Snacks/Bottled Drinks			
Breakfasts			
Lunches			
Dinners			
Groceries			
Bar/Pub			
Misc			
Total page 2			
Total page 1			
TOTAL			

TRAVEL
New Zealand
ITINERARY by VAN

Dates: _____

TRANSFER

Company: _____

Address: _____

_____

Phone: _____ Confirmation # _____

Notes: _____

FLIGHT

Airline: _____ Flight # _____

Location: _____ Reference # _____

Check in Time: _____ Departure Time: _____

Notes: _____

CAR HIRE/TRANSFER

Company: _____

Address: _____

_____

Phone: _____ Confirmation # _____

Notes _____

ACCOMMODATION

Name of Hotel: _____

Address: _____

_____

Phone: _____ Confirmation # _____

Notes: _____

TRAVEL
New Zealand
ITINERARY by VAN

Dates:

TRANSFER

Company:

Address:

Phone: Confirmation #

Notes:

FLIGHT

Airline: Flight #

Location: Reference #

Check in Time: Departure Time:

Notes:

CAR HIRE/TRANSFER

Company:

Address:

Phone: Confirmation #

Notes

ACCOMMODATION

Name of Hotel:

Address:

Phone: Confirmation #

Notes:

TRAVEL
New Zealand
ITINERARY by VAN

Dates: _____

TRANSFER

Company: _____

Address: _____

_____

Phone: _____ Confirmation # _____

Notes: _____

FLIGHT

Airline: _____ Flight # _____

Location: _____ Reference # _____

Check in Time: _____ Departure Time: _____

Notes: _____

CAR HIRE/TRANSFER

Company: _____

Address: _____

_____

Phone: _____ Confirmation # _____

Notes _____

ACCOMMODATION

Name of Hotel: _____

Address: _____

_____

Phone: _____ Confirmation # _____

Notes: _____

Dates:

TRANSFER

Company:

Address:

Phone: Confirmation #

Notes:

FLIGHT

Airline: Flight #

Location: Reference #

Check in Time: Departure Time:

Notes:

CAR HIRE/TRANSFER

Company:

Address:

Phone: Confirmation #

Notes

ACCOMMODATION

Name of Hotel:

Address:

Phone: Confirmation #

Notes:

TRAVEL
ITINERARY by VAN

Dates: _____

TRANSFER

Company: _____

Address: _____

_____

Phone: _____ Confirmation # _____

Notes: _____

FLIGHT

Airline: _____ Flight # _____

Location: _____ Reference # _____

Check in Time: _____ Departure Time: _____

Notes: _____

CAR HIRE/TRANSFER

Company: _____

Address: _____

_____

Phone: _____ Confirmation # _____

Notes _____

ACCOMMODATION

Name of Hotel: _____

Address: _____

_____

Phone: _____ Confirmation # _____

Notes: _____

TRAVEL
New Zealand
ITINERARY by VAN

Dates:

TRANSFER

Company:

Address:

Phone: Confirmation #

Notes:

FLIGHT

Airline: Flight #

Location: Reference #

Check in Time: Departure Time:

Notes:

CAR HIRE/TRANSFER

Company:

Address:

Phone: Confirmation #

Notes

ACCOMMODATION

Name of Hotel:

Address:

Phone: Confirmation #

Notes:

TRAVEL
ITINERARY by VAN

Dates: _____

TRANSFER

Company: _____

Address: _____

_____

Phone: _____ Confirmation # _____

Notes: _____

FLIGHT

Airline: _____ Flight # _____

Location: _____ Reference # _____

Check in Time: _____ Departure Time: _____

Notes: _____

CAR HIRE/TRANSFER

Company: _____

Address: _____

_____

Phone: _____ Confirmation # _____

Notes _____

ACCOMMODATION

Name of Hotel: _____

Address: _____

_____

Phone: _____ Confirmation # _____

Notes: _____

TRAVEL
DAY PLANNER by VAN

PRIORITY	MONDAY	TUESDAY	WEDNESDAY

THURSDAY	FRIDAY	SATURDAY	SUNDAY

PRIORITY	MONDAY	TUESDAY	WEDNESDAY

TRAVEL

DAY PLANNER ᵇʸ VAN

THURSDAY	FRIDAY	SATURDAY	SUNDAY

TRAVEL
New Zealand
DAY PLANNER _by_ VAN

PRIORITY	MONDAY	TUESDAY	WEDNESDAY

TRAVEL
DAY PLANNER by VAN

THURSDAY	FRIDAY	SATURDAY	SUNDAY

TRAVEL
DAY PLANNER by VAN

PRIORITY	MONDAY	TUESDAY	WEDNESDAY

TRAVEL
New Zealand
DAY PLANNER   by VAN

THURSDAY	FRIDAY	SATURDAY	SUNDAY

_____

_____

TRAVEL
New Zealand
PACKING LIST by VAN

CLOTHING	
Basics	**Casual**
☐	☐
☐	☐
☐	☐
☐	☐
☐	☐
☐	☐
☐	☐
Dressy	**Outerwear**
☐	☐
☐	☐
☐	☐
☐	☐
☐	☐
☐	☐
☐	☐
Accessories	**Wearing**
☐	☐
☐	☐
☐	☐
☐	☐
☐	☐

TRAVEL
New Zealand
PACKING LIST by VAN

Toiletries	Medication
☐	☐
☐	☐
☐	☐
☐	☐
☐	☐

Tech/Gear	Entertainment
☐	☐
☐	☐
☐	☐
☐	☐
☐	☐

Other	Food/Snacks
☐	☐
☐	☐
☐	☐
☐	☐

Travel Docs	Carry On
☐	☐
☐	☐
☐	☐
☐	☐
☐	☐

1-MONTH BEFORE	2-WEEKS BEFORE
☐	☐
☐	☐
☐	☐
☐	☐
☐	☐
☐	☐

1-WEEK BEFORE	2-DAYS BEFORE
☐	☐
☐	☐
☐	☐
☐	☐
☐	☐
☐	☐

24-HOURS BEFORE	DAY OF TRAVEL
☐	☐
☐	☐
☐	☐
☐	☐
☐	☐
☐	☐

TRAVEL New Zealand

CONVERSIONS by VAN

Date:

LENGTH

1 centimetre (cm)	=	10 millimetres (mm)
1 inch	=	2.54 centimetres (cm)
1 foot	=	0.3048 metres (m)
1 foot	=	12 inches
1 yard	=	3 feet
1 metre (m)	=	100 centimetres (cm)
1 metre (m)	=	3.280839895 feet
1 furlong	=	660 feet
1 kilometre (km)	=	1000 metres (m)
1 kilometre (km)	=	0.62137119 miles
1 mile	=	5280 ft
1 mile	=	1.609344 kilometres (km)
1 nautical mile	=	1.852 kilometres (km)

WEIGHT

1 milligram (mg)	=	0.001 grams (g)
1 gram (g)	=	0.001 kilograms (kg)
1 gram (g)	=	0.035273962 ounces
1 ounce	=	28.34952312 grams (g)
1 ounce	=	0.0625 pounds
1 pound (lb)	=	16 ounces
1 pound (lb)	=	0.45359237 kilograms (kg)
1 kilogram (kg)	=	1000 grams
1 kilogram (kg)	=	35.273962 ounces
1 kilogram (kg)	=	2.20462262 pounds (lb)
1 stone	=	14 pounds
1 short ton	=	2000 pounds
1 metric ton	=	1000 kilograms (kg)

AREA

1 square foot	=	144 square inches
1 square foot	=	929.0304 sq centimetres
1 square yard	=	9 square feet
1 square metre	=	10.7639104 square feet
1 acre	=	43,560 square feet
1 hectare	=	10,000 square metres
1 hectare	=	2.4710538 acres
1 sq kilometre	=	100 hectares
1 sq mile	=	2.58998811 sq kilometres
1 sq mile	=	640 acres

SPEED

1 mph	=	1.46666667 fps
1 mph	=	1.609344 kph
1 knot	=	1.150779448 mph
1 foot per second	=	0.68181818 mph (mph)
1 kph	=	0.62137119 mph

VOLUME

1 US tablespoon	=	3 US teaspoons
1 US fluid ounce	=	29.57353 milliliters (ml)
1 US cup	=	16 US tablespoons
1 US cup	=	8 US fluid ounces
1 US pint	=	2 US cups
1 US pint	=	16 US fluid ounces
1 litre (l)	=	33.8140227 US fl ounces
1 litre (l)	=	1000 milliliters (ml)
1 US quart	=	2 US pints
1 US gallon	=	4 US quarts
1 US gallon	=	3.78541178 litres

TEMPERATURE

Fahrenheit / Celcius

Fahrenheit	Celcius
130	55
120	50
110	45
100	40
90	35
80	30
70	25
60	20
50	15
40	10
30	5
20	0
10	-5
0	-10
-10	-15
-20	-20
-30	-25
	-30
	-35

TRAVEL

NOTES

by VAN

TRAVEL

by VAN

BON VOYAGE!

NOW, TURN THE PLANNER OVER AND
RECORD YOUR JOURNEY IN THE 32-DAY JOURNAL

FUEL LOG by VAN

Currency:

DATE	ODOMETER	LITRES	COST

TRAVEL

FUEL LOG by VAN

Currency:

DATE	ODOMETER	LITRES	COST

TRAVEL

EXPENSE LOG by VAN

Currency:

ATE	VENDOR	DESCRIPTION	AMOUNT

TRAVEL
New Zealand
EXPENSE LOG ʸ ⱽᴬᴺ

Currency: _____

DATE	VENDOR	DESCRIPTION	AMOUNT

Date:

Date:

SCHEDULE	SITESEEING
9:00	
9:30	
10:00	
10:30	
11:00	
11:30	
12:00	
12:30	WEATHER
1:00	
1:30	
2:00	
2:30	SPENDING MONEY

	BUDGET	SPENT	REMAINING
3:00			
3:30			
4:00			

SCHEDULE	NOTES
4:30	
5:00	
5:30	

EAT

B	
L	
D	

Date:

TRAVEL
New Zealand
TRAVEL DIARY by VAN

Date:

SCHEDULE	SITESEEING
9:00	
9:30	
10:00	
10:30	
11:00	
11:30	
12:00	

WEATHER

SCHEDULE	
12:30	
1:00	
1:30	
2:00	

SPENDING MONEY

BUDGET	SPENT	REMAINING

SCHEDULE
2:30
3:00
3:30
4:00

NOTES

SCHEDULE
4:30
5:00
5:30

EAT

B	
L	
D	

TRAVEL DIARY by VAN

Date: _____

TRAVEL
TRAVEL DIARY by VAN

Date:

SCHEDULE	SITESEEING

9:00

9:30

10:00

10:30

11:00

11:30

12:00

12:30

1:00

1:30

2:00

2:30

3:00

3:30

4:00

4:30

5:00

5:30

WEATHER

SPENDING MONEY

BUDGET	SPENT	REMAINING

NOTES

EAT

B

L

D

Date:

TRAVEL
New Zealand
TRAVEL DIARY by VAN

Date:

SCHEDULE	SITESEEING

9:00

9:30

10:00

10:30

11:00

11:30

12:00

12:30

1:00

1:30

2:00

2:30

3:00

3:30

4:00

4:30

5:00

5:30

WEATHER

SPENDING MONEY

BUDGET	SPENT	REMAINING

NOTES

EAT

B

L

D

Date:

TRAVEL DIARY by VAN

Date:

SCHEDULE	SITESEEING

SCHEDULE

9:00

9:30

10:00

10:30

11:00

11:30

12:00

12:30

1:00

1:30

2:00

2:30

3:00

3:30

4:00

4:30

5:00

5:30

SITESEEING

WEATHER

SPENDING MONEY

BUDGET	SPENT	REMAINING

NOTES

EAT

B

L

D

TRAVEL DIARY by VAN

Date:

TRAVEL
New Zealand
TRAVEL DIARY by **VAN**

Date:

SCHEDULE	SITESEEING
9:00	
9:30	
10:00	
10:30	
11:00	
11:30	
12:00	
12:30	**WEATHER**
1:00	
1:30	
2:00	
2:30	**SPENDING MONEY**

	BUDGET	SPENT	REMAINING
3:00			
3:30			
4:00			

NOTES

4:30

5:00

5:30

EAT

B

L

D

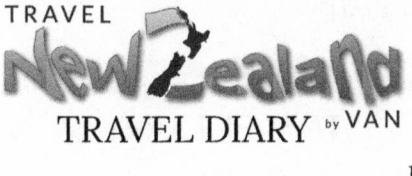

TRAVEL DIARY by VAN

Date: _____

_____

_____
_____
_____
_____
_____
_____
_____
_____
_____
_____
_____
_____
_____
_____
_____
_____
_____
_____
_____
_____
_____
_____
_____
_____
_____
_____
_____

TRAVEL DIARY by VAN

Date:

SCHEDULE	SITESEEING

9:00

9:30

10:00

10:30

11:00

11:30

12:00

12:30

WEATHER

1:00

1:30

2:00

2:30

SPENDING MONEY

BUDGET	SPENT	REMAINING

3:00

3:30

4:00

4:30

NOTES

5:00

5:30

EAT

B

L

D

TRAVEL
TRAVEL DIARY by VAN

Date: _____

_____

_____

_____

_____

_____

_____

_____

_____

_____

_____

_____

_____

_____

_____

_____

_____

_____

_____

_____

_____

_____

_____

_____

_____

_____

_____

_____

_____

TRAVEL
New Zealand
TRAVEL DIARY by VAN

Date:

SCHEDULE	SITESEEING
9:00	
9:30	
10:00	
10:30	
11:00	
11:30	
12:00	
12:30	**WEATHER**
1:00	
1:30	
2:00	
2:30	**SPENDING MONEY**

BUDGET	SPENT	REMAINING

SCHEDULE	
3:00	
3:30	
4:00	
4:30	**NOTES**
5:00	
5:30	

EAT

B	
L	
D	

Date:

Date:

SCHEDULE	SITESEEING
9:00	
9:30	
10:00	
10:30	
11:00	
11:30	
12:00	

WEATHER

12:30	
1:00	
1:30	
2:00	

SPENDING MONEY

	BUDGET	SPENT	REMAINING
2:30			
3:00			
3:30			
4:00			

NOTES

4:30	
5:00	
5:30	

EAT

B	
L	
D	

Date:

TRAVEL

TRAVEL DIARY by VAN

Date:

SCHEDULE	SITESEEING

9:00

9:30

10:00

10:30

11:00

11:30

12:00

12:30   **WEATHER**

1:00

1:30

2:00

2:30   **SPENDING MONEY**

BUDGET	SPENT	REMAINING

3:00

3:30

4:00

4:30   **NOTES**

5:00

5:30

EAT

B

L

D

TRAVEL DIARY by VAN

Date: _____

_____

_____

_____

_____

_____

_____

_____

_____

_____

_____

_____

_____

_____

_____

_____

_____

_____

_____

_____

_____

_____

_____

_____

_____

_____

_____

TRAVEL DIARY by VAN

Date:

SCHEDULE	SITESEEING

9:00

9:30

10:00

10:30

11:00

11:30

12:00

12:30

1:00

1:30

2:00

2:30

3:00

3:30

4:00

4:30

5:00

5:30

WEATHER

SPENDING MONEY

BUDGET	SPENT	REMAINING

NOTES

EAT

B

L

D

_____

_____

_____

_____

_____

_____

_____

_____

_____

_____

_____

_____

_____

_____

_____

_____

_____

_____

_____

_____

_____

_____

_____

_____

_____

_____

_____

_____

_____

_____

_____

_____

_____

_____

_____

TRAVEL DIARY by **VAN**

Date:

SCHEDULE	SITESEEING
9:00	
9:30	
10:00	
10:30	
11:00	
11:30	
12:00	

WEATHER

SCHEDULE	
12:30	
1:00	
1:30	
2:00	

SPENDING MONEY

BUDGET	SPENT	REMAINING

2:30
3:00
3:30
4:00

NOTES

4:30
5:00
5:30

EAT

B	
L	
D	

TRAVEL

TRAVEL DIARY by VAN

Date:

TRAVEL

New Zealand

TRAVEL DIARY by **VAN**

Date:

SCHEDULE	SITESEEING
9:00	
9:30	
10:00	
10:30	
11:00	
11:30	
12:00	
12:30	**WEATHER**
1:00	
1:30	
2:00	
2:30	**SPENDING MONEY**

BUDGET	SPENT	REMAINING

SCHEDULE
3:00
3:30
4:00
4:30
5:00
5:30

NOTES

EAT

B	
L	
D	

Date:

SCHEDULE	SITESEEING
9:00	
9:30	
10:00	
10:30	
11:00	
11:30	
12:00	
12:30	**WEATHER**
1:00	
1:30	
2:00	
2:30	**SPENDING MONEY**

	BUDGET	SPENT	REMAINING
3:00			
3:30			
4:00			

4:30	NOTES
5:00	
5:30	

EAT

B	
L	
D	

TRAVEL
NEW Zealand
TRAVEL DIARY by VAN

Date:

TRAVEL

TRAVEL DIARY by **VAN**

Date:

SCHEDULE	SITESEEING

9:00	
9:30	
10:00	
10:30	
11:00	
11:30	
12:00	

WEATHER

12:30	
1:00	
1:30	
2:00	

SPENDING MONEY

BUDGET	SPENT	REMAINING

2:30	
3:00	
3:30	
4:00	

NOTES

4:30	
5:00	
5:30	

EAT

B	
L	
D	

Date:

TRAVEL
TRAVEL DIARY by VAN

Date:

SCHEDULE	SITESEEING
9:00	
9:30	
10:00	
10:30	
11:00	
11:30	
12:00	
12:30	**WEATHER**
1:00	
1:30	
2:00	
2:30	**SPENDING MONEY**
3:00	BUDGET / SPENT / REMAINING
3:30	
4:00	
4:30	**NOTES**
5:00	
5:30	

EAT

B

L

D

TRAVEL
New Zealand
TRAVEL DIARY by VAN

Date:

Date:

SCHEDULE	SITESEEING
9:00	
9:30	
10:00	
10:30	
11:00	
11:30	
12:00	
12:30	**WEATHER**
1:00	
1:30	
2:00	
2:30	**SPENDING MONEY**

BUDGET	SPENT	REMAINING

3:00	
3:30	
4:00	
4:30	**NOTES**
5:00	
5:30	

EAT

B	
L	
D	

Date: _____

TRAVEL DIARY by VAN

Date:

SCHEDULE	SITESEEING
9:00	
9:30	
10:00	
10:30	
11:00	
11:30	
12:00	
12:30	WEATHER
1:00	
1:30	
2:00	
2:30	SPENDING MONEY
3:00	
3:30	
4:00	
4:30	NOTES
5:00	
5:30	

SPENDING MONEY

BUDGET	SPENT	REMAINING

NOTES

EAT

B	
L	
D	

Date:

Date:

SCHEDULE	SITESEEING
9:00	
9:30	
10:00	
10:30	
11:00	
11:30	
12:00	
12:30	**WEATHER**
1:00	
1:30	
2:00	
2:30	**SPENDING MONEY**

	BUDGET	SPENT	REMAINING
3:00			
3:30			
4:00			

SCHEDULE	NOTES
4:30	
5:00	
5:30	

EAT

B	
L	
D	

TRAVEL DIARY by VAN

Date: _____

TRAVEL
New Zealand
TRAVEL DIARY by VAN

Date:

SCHEDULE	SITESEEING

9:00

9:30

10:00

10:30

11:00

11:30

12:00

12:30   **WEATHER**

1:00

1:30

2:00

2:30   **SPENDING MONEY**

BUDGET	SPENT	REMAINING

3:00

3:30

4:00

4:30   **NOTES**

5:00

5:30

EAT

B

L

D

TRAVEL DIARY by VAN

Date: _____

TRAVEL DIARY by VAN

Date:

SCHEDULE	SITESEEING
9:00	
9:30	
10:00	
10:30	
11:00	
11:30	
12:00	
12:30	**WEATHER**
1:00	
1:30	
2:00	
2:30	**SPENDING MONEY**

BUDGET	SPENT	REMAINING

SCHEDULE	
3:00	
3:30	
4:00	
4:30	**NOTES**
5:00	
5:30	

EAT

B	
L	
D	

Date:

SCHEDULE	SITESEEING
9:00	
9:30	
10:00	
10:30	
11:00	
11:30	
12:00	
12:30	**WEATHER**
1:00	
1:30	
2:00	
2:30	**SPENDING MONEY**

	BUDGET	SPENT	REMAINING
3:00			
3:30			
4:00			

SCHEDULE	NOTES
4:30	
5:00	
5:30	

EAT

B	
L	
D	

Date:

New Zealand
TRAVEL DIARY by VAN

Date: _____

SCHEDULE	SITESEEING

SCHEDULE

9:00 _____

9:30 _____

10:00 _____

10:30 _____

11:00 _____

11:30 _____

12:00 _____

12:30 _____

1:00 _____

1:30 _____

2:00 _____

2:30 _____

3:00 _____

3:30 _____

4:00 _____

4:30 _____

5:00 _____

5:30 _____

EAT

B _____

L _____

D _____

SITESEEING

WEATHER

SPENDING MONEY

BUDGET	SPENT	REMAINING

NOTES

TRAVEL DIARY by VAN

Date:

Date:

SCHEDULE	SITESEEING

9:00

9:30

10:00

10:30

11:00

11:30

12:00

12:30

WEATHER

1:00

1:30

2:00

2:30

SPENDING MONEY

BUDGET	SPENT	REMAINING

3:00

3:30

4:00

4:30

NOTES

5:00

5:30

EAT

B

L

D

Date:

Date:

SCHEDULE	SITESEEING
9:00	
9:30	
10:00	
10:30	
11:00	
11:30	
12:00	
12:30	WEATHER
1:00	
1:30	
2:00	
2:30	SPENDING MONEY
3:00	
3:30	
4:00	
4:30	NOTES
5:00	
5:30	

SPENDING MONEY

BUDGET	SPENT	REMAINING

EAT

B	
L	
D	

TRAVEL
New Zealand
TRAVEL DIARY by VAN

Date:

TRAVEL DIARY by VAN

Date:

SCHEDULE	SITESEEING

9:00

9:30

10:00

10:30

11:00

11:30

12:00

12:30

1:00

1:30

2:00

2:30

3:00

3:30

4:00

4:30

5:00

5:30

WEATHER

SPENDING MONEY

BUDGET	SPENT	REMAINING

NOTES

EAT

B

L

D

TRAVEL DIARY by VAN

Date:

TRAVEL DIARY by VAN

Date:

SCHEDULE	SITESEEING
9:00	
9:30	
10:00	
10:30	
11:00	
11:30	
12:00	
12:30	**WEATHER**
1:00	
1:30	
2:00	
2:30	**SPENDING MONEY**

BUDGET	SPENT	REMAINING

SCHEDULE	
3:00	
3:30	
4:00	
4:30	**NOTES**
5:00	
5:30	

EAT

B	
L	
D	

Date:

Date:

SCHEDULE	SITESEEING
9:00	
9:30	
10:00	
10:30	
11:00	
11:30	
12:00	
12:30	**WEATHER**
1:00	
1:30	
2:00	
2:30	**SPENDING MONEY**

BUDGET	SPENT	REMAINING

SCHEDULE	
3:00	
3:30	
4:00	

NOTES

SCHEDULE	
4:30	
5:00	
5:30	

EAT

B	
L	
D	

TRAVEL

TRAVEL DIARY by VAN

Date:

TRAVEL

TRAVEL DIARY by VAN

Date:

SCHEDULE	SITESEEING
9:00	
9:30	
10:00	
10:30	
11:00	
11:30	
12:00	
12:30	**WEATHER**
1:00	
1:30	
2:00	
2:30	**SPENDING MONEY**

	BUDGET	SPENT	REMAINING
3:00			
3:30			
4:00			

NOTES

4:30

5:00

5:30

EAT

B

L

D

TRAVEL DIARY by VAN

Date:

TRAVEL
New Zealand
TRAVEL DIARY by VAN

Date:

SCHEDULE	SITESEEING
9:00	
9:30	
10:00	
10:30	
11:00	
11:30	
12:00	
12:30	**WEATHER**
1:00	
1:30	
2:00	
2:30	**SPENDING MONEY**

	BUDGET	SPENT	REMAINING
3:00			
3:30			
4:00			

4:30	**NOTES**
5:00	
5:30	

EAT

B	
L	
D	

TRAVEL DIARY by VAN

Date: _____

TRAVEL
New Zealand
TRAVEL DIARY by VAN

Date:

SCHEDULE	SITESEEING
9:00	
9:30	
10:00	
10:30	
11:00	
11:30	
12:00	

SCHEDULE

9:00

9:30

10:00

10:30

11:00

11:30

12:00

12:30

1:00

1:30

2:00

2:30

3:00

3:30

4:00

4:30

5:00

5:30

EAT

B

L

D

SITESEEING

WEATHER

SPENDING MONEY

BUDGET	SPENT	REMAINING

NOTES

WELCOME TO YOUR

TRAVEL

by VAN

PLANNER & DIARY

Made in the USA
Las Vegas, NV
14 December 2022

62146354R00059